FROM Egg TO Butterfly

SHANNON ZEMLICKA

 LERNER PUBLICATIONS COMPANY Minneapolis

Lerner Publications Company
A division of Lerner Publishing Group, Inc.
241 First Avenue North
Minneapolis, MN 55401 U.S.A.

Website address: www.lernerbooks.com

Photo Acknowledgments
The images in this book are used with the permission of:
© Robert Pickett/Papilio/Alamy, p. 1; © iStockphoto.com/
Terry J. Alcorn, p. 3; © Ken Thomas/Photo Researchers,
Inc., p. 5; © James H. Robbison/Photo Researchers, Inc.,
p. 7; © Brian Kenney/Oxford Scientific/Photolibrary, p. 9;
© Silvia Reiche/Minden Pictures, p. 11; © Dick Poe/Visuals
Unlimited, Inc., p. 13; © Robert & Jean Pollock/Visuals
Unlimited, Inc., p. 15; © Ingo Arndt/Minden Pictures,
p. 17; © Kathleen Blanchard/Visuals Unlimited, Inc., p. 19;
© Biosphoto/Tiziana Bertani, p. 21; © Jim McKinley/Flickr/
Getty Images, p. 23.

Front Cover: © James Laurie/Shutterstock Images.

Main body text set in Arta Std Book 20/26.
Typeface provided by International Typeface Corp.

Library of Congress Cataloging-in-Publication Data

Knudsen, Shannon, 1971–
        From egg to butterfly / by Shannon Zemlicka.
            p.   cm. — (Start to finish, second series. Nature's cycles)
        Includes index.
        ISBN 978-0-7613-6562-4 (lib. bdg. : alk. paper)
        1. Butterflies—Life cycles—Juvenile literature.
    I. Title.
    QL544.2.K76 2012
    595.78'9—dc23   2011024562

Manufactured in the United States of America
1 – DP – 12/31/11

TABLE OF Contents

Look! A butterfly! How does a butterfly grow?

A mother lays eggs.

A butterfly starts as an egg. A mother butterfly lays her eggs on a plant. This picture shows eggs close up. The eggs are really tiny.

The eggs hatch.

Sometimes the eggs grow for a few days. Other times, they grow for months. Then they hatch. A **caterpillar** comes out of each egg. A caterpillar looks like a fat worm with legs.

The caterpillar eats.

The caterpillar is hungry. It eats its eggshell. Then it eats green plants.

The caterpillar grows.

Eating makes the caterpillar grow. It gets bigger and bigger. But its skin does not grow. The skin becomes very tight. It fits like a coat that is too small.

The caterpillar sheds its skin.

The caterpillar's skin splits open. A new skin grows under it. The new skin fits just right. The caterpillar wriggles out of the old skin. This is called **molting**.

A shell forms.

The caterpillar grows and molts, grows and molts. Then it hangs from a branch. It molts again. This time, a hard shell forms around it. The caterpillar has become a **pupa**.

The body changes.

The pupa stays inside the shell. It grows and changes. Wings form. What is happening?

The shell cracks.

The pupa has turned into a butterfly. Its body cracks the shell. The butterfly crawls out. It is soft and wet.

Wings open.

The butterfly rests. It opens its wings slowly. Sun and air dry the wings.

Fly, fly away!

The butterfly is ready to fly. It has grown from egg to butterfly!

Glossary

caterpillar (KAT-ur-pill-ur): a butterfly's form early in its life

hatch (HACH): break open

molting (MOHL-ting): shedding skin

pupa (PYOO-puh): a butterfly's form after it is a caterpillar

Index